D1164907

Period.

A GIRL'S GUIDE TO MENSTRUATION
with
A Parent's Guide

REVISED and UPDATED

JoAnn Loulan
Bonnie Worthen

Illustrated by Chris Wold Dyrud & Marcia Quackenbush

BOOK PEDDLERS
Minnetonka, MN
distributed to the US book trade by PGW

ISBN 0-916773-97-3 (hardcover, library edition)
ISBN 0-916773-96-5 (paperback with removeable Parent's Guide)

Publisher's Cataloging-in-Publication Data
(Provided by Quality Books, Inc.)

Loulan, JoAnn.
Period : a girl's guide to menstruation : with a parent's guide / JoAnn Loulan, Bonnie Worthen ; illustrated by Chris Wold Dyrud & Marcia Quackenbush. --Book Peddlers ed., rev. and updated.
p.cm.
SUMMARY: Discusses the physical and psychological changes at the onset of menstruation.
Includes index.
ISBN: 0-916773-97-3 (hbk.)
ISBN: 0-916773-96-5 (pbk.)

1. Menstruation--Juvenile literature.
I. Lopez, Bonnie. II. Dryud, Chris Wold.
III. Quackenbush, Marcia. IV. Title.

QP263.L68 2000 612.6'62
QBI00-461

You can also order directly from the publisher:
BOOK PEDDLERS, 15245 Minnetonka Blvd, Minnetonka, MN 55345
(800) 255-3379 • (952) 912-0036 • fax (952) 912-0105
www.bookpeddlers.com

Schools, Agencies, Organizations: Contact us directly for quantity discount rates.

book trade distributor: Publishers Group West

Printed in Hong Kong

01 02 03 04 05 10 9 8 7 6 5 4 3 2 1

Contents

introduction

Three women, JoAnn Gardener-Loulan, Bonnie Lopez-Worthen, and Marcia Quackenbush wrote this book in 1979 for girls who are growing up. They thought it would be important to have a book explaining some of the changes all girls go through. They talked about all kinds of things as they wrote this book and included many of the experiences of their friends. What they said then, is still true now. Our questions and our concerns are much the same today.

This is a chance for us all to learn from each other.

BUS

CHAPTER ONE

So Many Changes

Magazines, billboards, television and movies show girls and women who are tall and slim, have faces with no pimples, never wear glasses and seem to have no big problems at all. Not too many people really are that way, but when we see so many women like that it can make us feel that somehow our body or face or hair is just not right.

We live in a crazy, mixed-up world because many girls and women think that everyone else has the longest hair or smallest feet, nicest smile or prettiest eyes. We were never created to look alike or to look like somebody else. What most people have in common is that we have bodies that can do many wonderful and different things, no matter what color, size or shape we are.

We can walk or read or sing or take bubble baths; we can taste wonderful foods or throw balls or listen to birds chirping or dance or run or think or laugh. Sometimes bodies can make us feel *sooooooo..... good!*

One reason we all have different bodies is because of our mother and father. They have passed some things about their bodies on to us, like the color of our eyes, skin and hair, or how tall we are. You might have your mother's hair color and your father's eyes.

Sometimes we think we really can't be happy unless we look like our favorite movie star or girlfriend or aunt. Being comfortable with your own body is important. Learning to love your own specialness is a big part of growing up.

Some of us have bodies that are disabled. This means that some part of the body can't be moved (is *paralyzed*) or moves uncontrollably (is *spastic*). Maybe we are blind or deaf, or we have one leg or arm that didn't grow as long as the other. Or a part of our body had to be removed (*amputated*) because something was wrong with it. Lots of people have these kinds of bodies and it's important that we all learn to appreciate the wonderful things our bodies can do for us. Disabled people can do things that "able-bodied" people can't. "Able-bodied" people can do things disabled people can't. This doesn't mean one person is better than another, it just means that we're different.

Since your birth, your body has been changing and growing. When you get to be ten or twelve or fourteen, more obvious changes begin to happen. You may begin getting pimples, and the hair under your arms and on your legs may be easier to see. Some people start to sweat (*perspire*), and perspiration may smell different as you grow older. Your hips get bigger, your body actually begins to change shape and your breasts begin to grow. And both breasts don't always grow at the same rate in the beginning. This is pretty common.

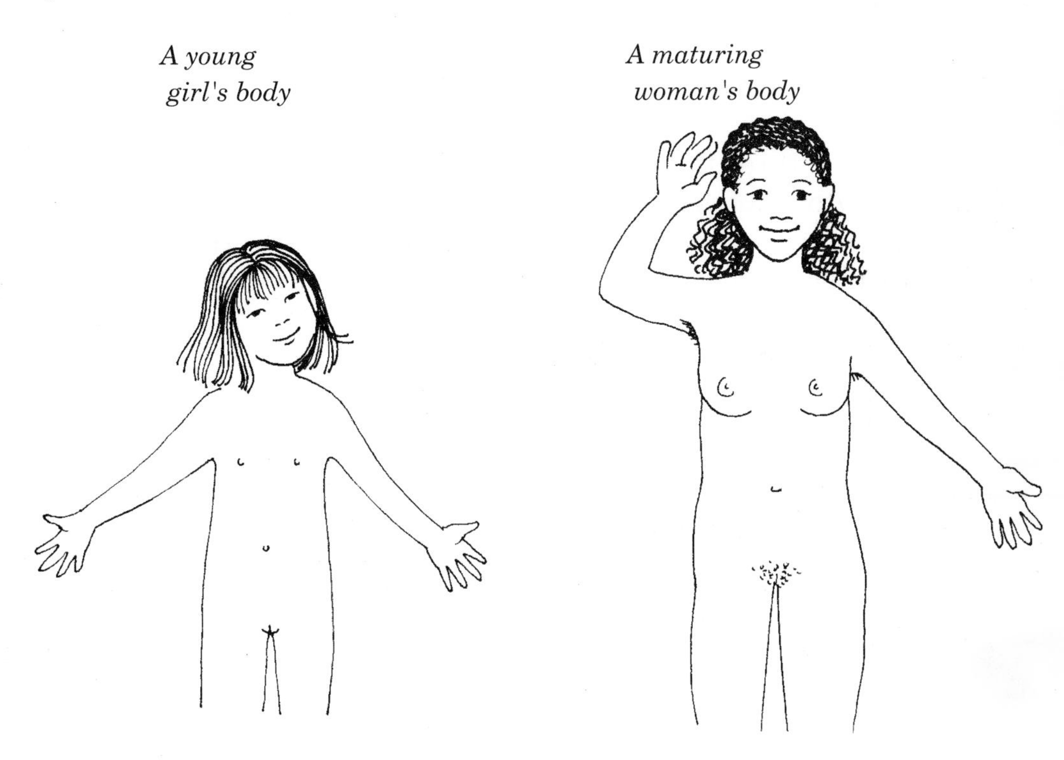

The area around your nipple, called the *areola* (ah-REE-oh-la), becomes a little raised and might change color. You might begin growing taller at this age. You will also probably start growing hair on the area below your belly button, close to your legs. This is called *pubic* (PEW-bik) *hair*.

It seems that all of a sudden you are running around with a new body, and it may take some getting used to. You may be the first one in school to show breasts or the last one to gain some weight and start looking older. Maybe your parents or older sisters and brothers will tease and embarrass you. Boys or other girls may make fun of your new bra. You may not believe this, but few of us are comfortable with these changes.

Can you think of three things you really like about your body? Do you like the color or softness of your skin? How about your legs or hands? Or smile? You really are a special person, and the more you realize that, the better you will feel about yourself.

"I Was Sure I Was Different."

"I used to drive myself crazy when I was growing up because I had no waist. Everyone I saw at school or on the street had tiny waists—everyone but me. So I would diet and not let myself eat things that everyone else ate. Do you know what happened? I lost weight and still had no waist! Then I finally caught on that I had a certain body type and no matter what I ate, I would just go from my rib cage to my hips in a straight line. I am feeling much better about myself just knowing everyone has a different body."

"I used to hate the hair on my upper lip. My hair is black, so it's really noticeable. Then I met a girl at school who was just like me and I would watch her when the kids teased her. It really surprised me because it didn't bother her at all! That's when I stopped worrying."

"When I was growing pubic hair, I thought something was wrong with me so I began pulling it out with tweezers. I realized it was normal when I just couldn't pull it out fast enough. But it sure was scary at first!"

CHAPTER TWO

So Many Parts

Some of the changes your body goes through as you grow older are easy to see, but others go on inside of your body. Even though you don't usually see these changes, they affect your life and the way you feel.

There are several diagrams in this book which will help explain things, but remember that every woman is different and none of the diagrams will really be exactly like you or anyone else. They can give you an idea of shapes and where things are.

There are quite a few organs inside of us. One way to look at them is by a "cross section" diagram. This is a cross section of an apple. You see the lines and shapes and seeds of the inside of the apple.

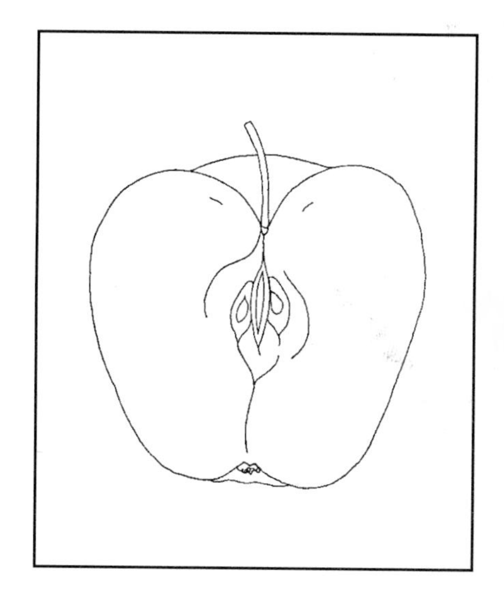

The internal organs we are talking about are organs that only girls and women have.

The body of a girl is different from that of a woman, but it's hard to say exactly when a girl becomes a woman. From the time we're born, our bodies start the kinds of changes this book is about. In a young girl, internal organs (organs that are inside of us) look something like this diagram.

This shows the size of a twelve-year-old girl's uterus.

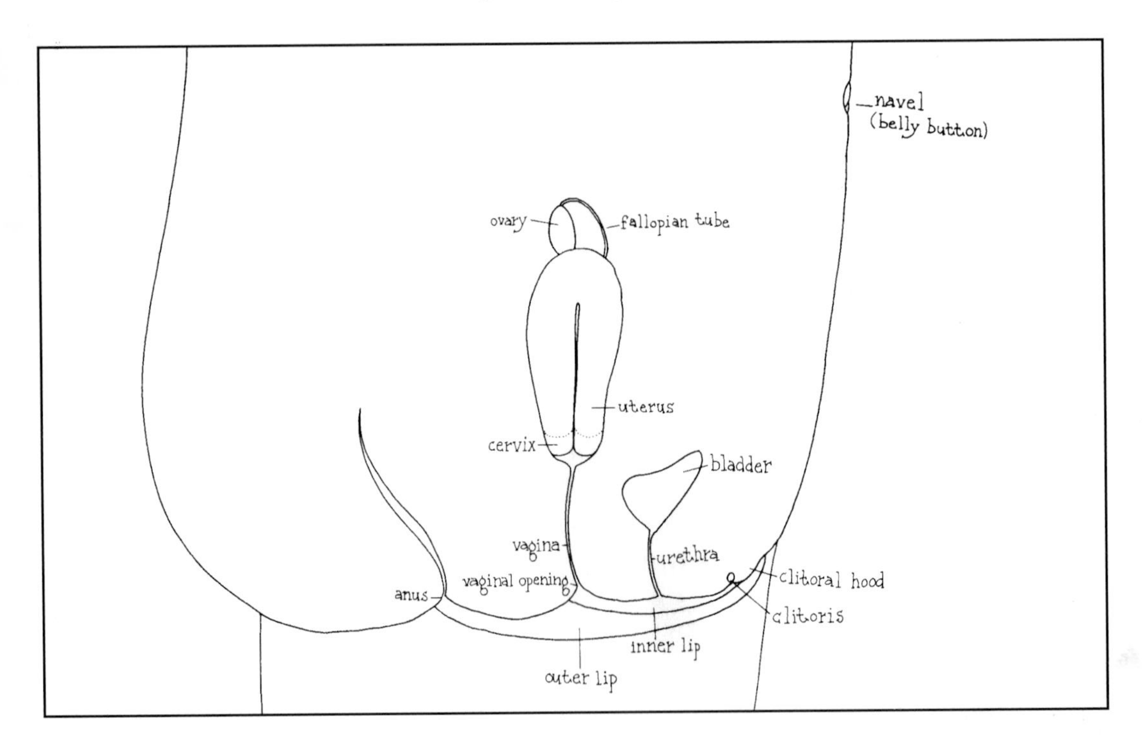

The uterus is an interesting organ. It seems like it should be very large since a baby might have to fit inside of it someday. But it really isn't big at all. It's about the size of your fist. When a woman becomes pregnant, the uterus grows in size with the baby, and after the baby is born, the uterus becomes small again.

This diagram is of a twenty-five year-old woman.

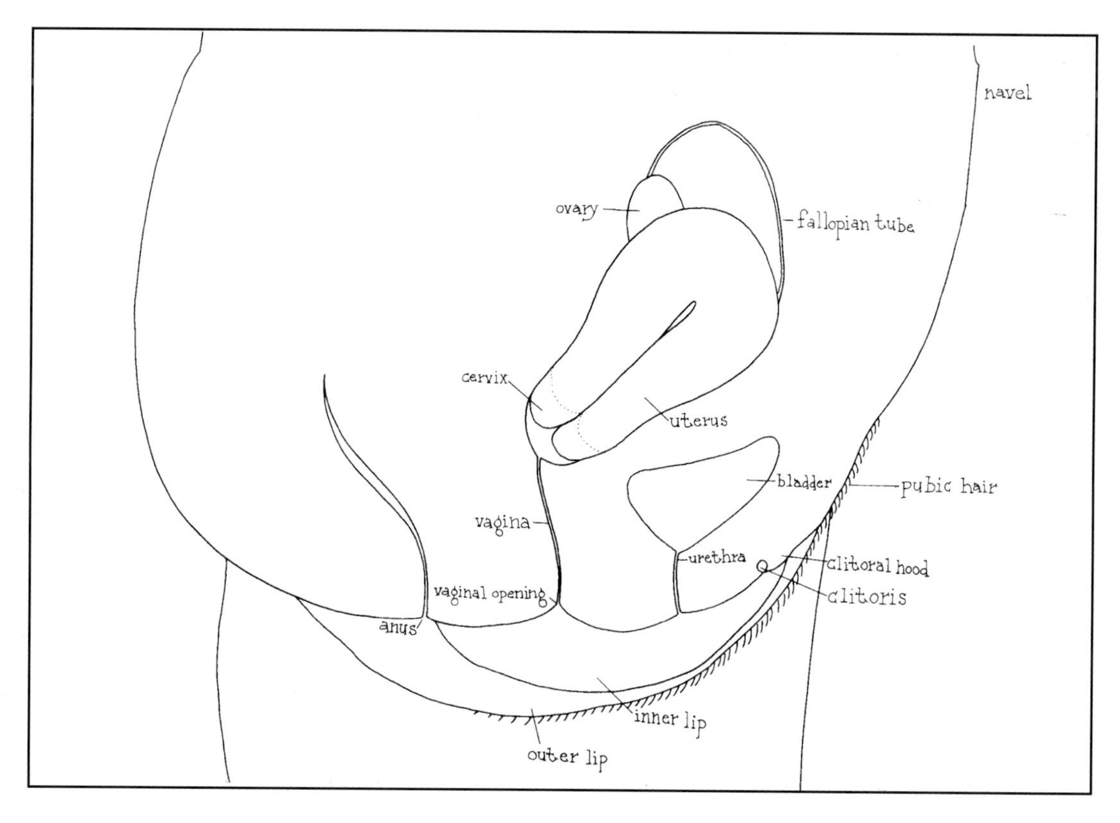

The vagina is another organ which seems like it should be larger because a baby has to travel through the vagina when it's being born. But during birth, the vagina stretches, then it shrinks back to normal just as the uterus does. The sides of the vagina, called the vaginal walls, usually lie close together, touching, like a balloon with no air in it.

Here is a list of some of these organs, what they are called and why we have them:

The *uterus* (YOU-ter-us) is where an egg grows into a baby when a woman is pregnant.

The *vagina* (va-JI-nah) is a passageway that leads from the uterus to the outside of the body.

The *vaginal opening* (VA-jin-al) is the opening leading into the vagina.

The *hymen* (HI-men) is a thin piece of skin that surrounds the opening to the vagina.

The *cervix* (SER-vix) protects delicate tissues in the uterus. It has an opening which leads from the uterus to the vagina. The opening of the cervix is only as big around as a piece of spaghetti.

The *ovaries* (OH-vah-reez) are the organs that hold all the *ova* (OH-vah) or the eggs. One egg is called an *ovum* (OH-vum). The cross section shows only one ovary, but in the front view diagram, you can see both. They hold many more eggs than are ever needed or used. When a baby girl is born, all those eggs are already in her little ovaries. Ovaries are sort of spongy and the eggs are tucked away in little pockets and folds. One egg is only as big as the tip of a needle.

Every so often, an egg travels from one ovary to the uterus. It moves along one of the *fallopian tubes* (fa-LOH-pee-an). *(This is explained more in the next chapter.)* Each fallopian tube is about four inches long and no bigger around than a piece of thread. These tubes are lined with very tiny little hairs. If you looked at the inside of one through a microscope, it would look like soft velvet.

The *urethra* (you-REE-thrah) is the opening where *urine* (YUR-rin) passes from the body.

The *bladder* (BLAD-der) is where your body holds urine until you go to the bathroom.

The *anus* (AY-nus) is the opening through which bowel movements pass.

The *inner lips* are folds of skin that surround the urethra and vaginal opening. The *outer lips* are pads of skin that protect the very delicate tissues in this area. When you get older, hair grows on your outer lips. This adds protection and is called *pubic* (PEW-bik) hair.

The *clitoris* (CLIT-tor-iss) is a small bump of skin. It's very sensitive because it contains many nerve endings. Because the clitoris is so sensitive, there is a cover to protect it. This is called the *clitoral hood*.

Genitals (JEN-a-tulls) refers to the entire area we've been talking about. The inner and outer lips, clitoris, urethra, vaginal opening and anus make up the genital area.

Even though some of our genitals are outside of our bodies, we don't see them very often. Like most parts of our bodies, genitals change as we get older, too, but often we don't notice. We rarely look at our genitals because they are tucked away. When you're young, it looks as if you don't have any inner lips at all. They're very small. When you're older, your inner lips grow larger, but exactly how much they grow is different for all of us.

Just like one's smile or the color of one's hair, everyone's genitals are a little different. So, however you are, is just the way you are suppose to be.

It might help to think of flowers or sea shells—no two flowers will ever be quite the same even if they're the same kind of flower.

CHAPTER THREE

Menstruation

One of the things that happens when a girl grows up is that she will begin to *menstruate* (MEN-stroo-ate). What exactly is this mysterious thing called *menstruation* (MEN-stroo-AY-shun)?

At a certain time in your life, maybe when you're ten, or twelve, or fifteen, the *hormones* (HOR-mones) in your body become very active. Hormones are chemicals your body makes. These hormones, in their own special way, begin telling your body to be alert, pay attention, and start doing things it's never done before. There are hundreds and hundreds of these messages. In this chapter, only a few will be mentioned. It would be confusing to try to keep track of all of them.

One of the first things to happen is that an egg works its way out of one of your ovaries. (Remember that this egg will be no larger than the point of a needle.) This tiny egg floating around wants to get from the ovary to the uterus. That seems a difficult thing to do, especially since the egg doesn't have any wings to fly with or wheels to roll with. But each fallopian tube has these teeny tiny little hairs at the end of it, almost like fingers. They swoosh back and forth like waves in the ocean, trying to help the egg inside the tube. When this happens, the egg travels all the way through the fallopian tube to the uterus.

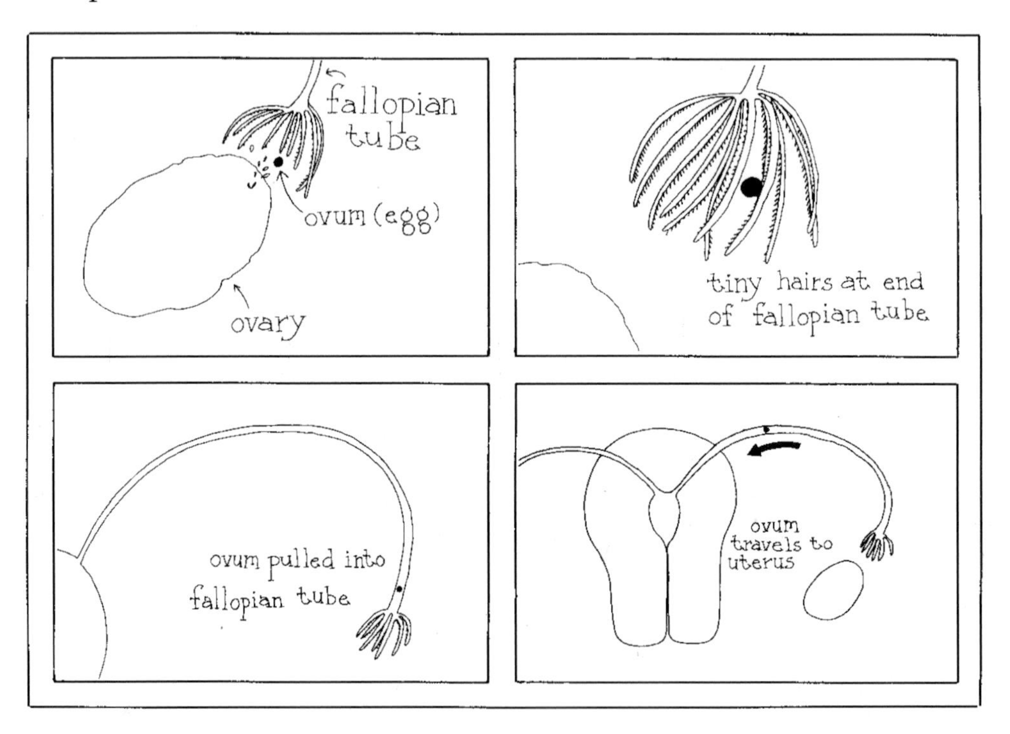

At the same time this happens, your uterus begins building up a lining of healthy fresh tissue and blood. (You can picture what a "lining" is if you think of wallpaper on the walls in a house.) By the time the egg reaches the uterus, the lining of the uterus is full and rich and soft. If the egg is going to stay for awhile and become a baby, this lining will make its stay healthy and comfortable. But, most of the time, the egg just visits and then passes on through. If the egg isn't staying in the uterus, the uterus doesn't need all that lining, so the lining, made up of blood and tiny pieces of tissue, dribbles out. It passes through the small opening in the cervix, down through the vagina and out the vaginal opening. About a month after the egg pops out of one of the ovaries, another egg does the same and the whole cycle starts again. This is what menstruation is all about.

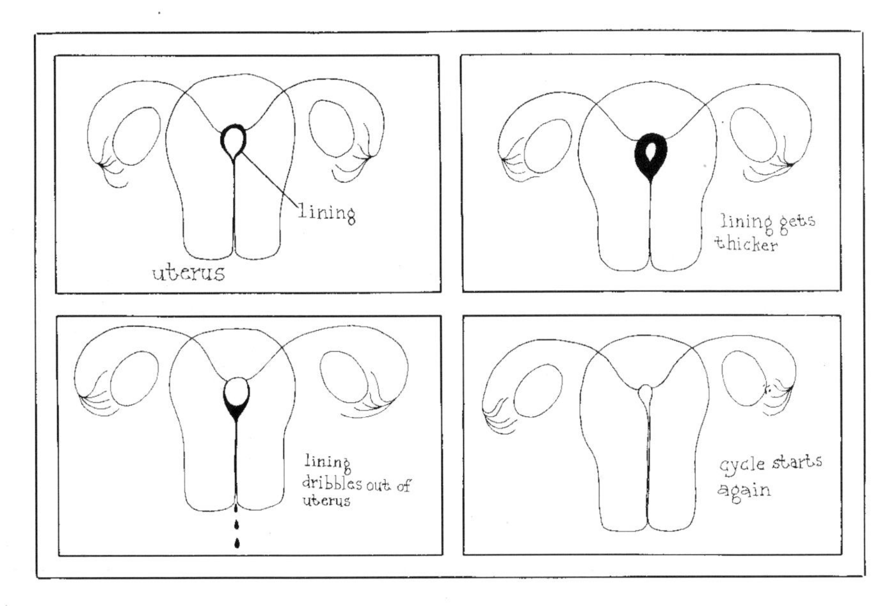

It seems like all this shouldn't take very long because everything is so busy. Actually, though, the whole menstrual cycle takes about a month. The part where your uterus is dribbling blood and lining may last anywhere from two to eight days. It's different for every girl and woman. Once you've started your menstrual cycle, the monthly dribbling of blood will probably keep happening until you're forty or fifty. Then those hormones will send different messages around and your body will stop menstruating. That time in a woman's life is called *menopause* (MEN-o-pause).

Something else that happens to many girls is that another kind of fluid comes out of their vagina before they get their first period. This is called a vaginal discharge. You will probably notice this on your underpants. There is usually not very much of it. It might be clear, thin and waterlike. It might be sticky and yellow or milky-white. This fluid or *mucous* (MU-cuss) may have a faint odor, or no odor at all. This is normal and healthy. You might notice this happening more than once before you get your period and it may occur just before each cycle after you begin getting your period.

If the vaginal discharge is a dark color (brown or green), and the smell is very strong, or you itch or burn in your vagina or around your outer lips, you should talk to a grown-up and see a doctor. You may just have a slight infection.

~PADS~
Tampons
Tampons
MINI PADS
REGULAR
Tampons regular
LONG SUPER PADS

CHAPTER FOUR

Pads or Tampons?

Until the early 1900's, girls and women placed folded pieces of cloth inside their underpants to catch their menstrual blood. Today we have so many menstrual products to choose from that it's almost hard to decide which is best to use. It will be easier to choose a product when you know what each is like and how it is used.

The general term for these products is feminine *hygiene* (HI-gene) or feminine care products. There are two main types of products: sanitary pads or napkins which collect the menstrual flow outside your body, and tampons which absorb menstrual flow inside your body.

SANITARY PADS or NAPKINS

The sanitary pad, first developed in the 1920's, comes in many different sizes and shapes. Pads are made of an absorbent material with a bottom, wet-proof shield to keep your menstrual flow from staining your pants and clothes.

It used to be that pads were held in place with a small elastic belt called a sanitary belt.

The belt looked like this:

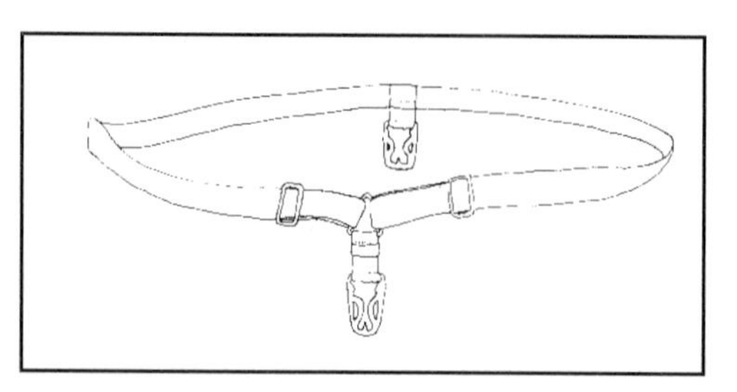

The pad was fastened to it like this:

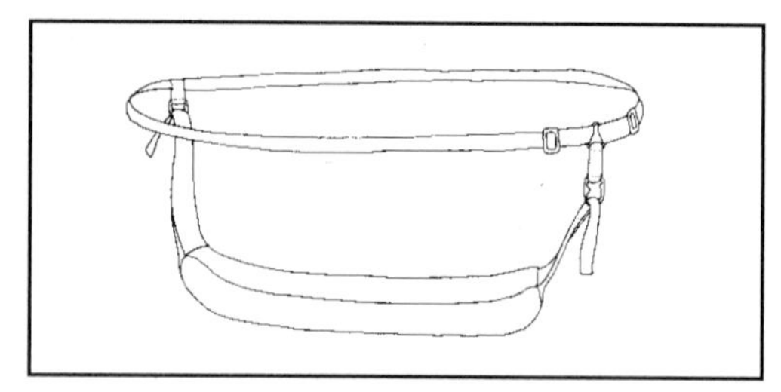

It is possible that your mother used a sanitary belt. It is certainly true that your grandmother did. Ask them.

Today pads are made to be worn without belts. They have a sticky strip that keeps them in place on your underpants. One side of a pad faces toward your body and one toward your underpants. You remove a strip of paper that exposes the adhesive and you stick that to your underwear. When it's time to replace it, the pad pulls off easily.

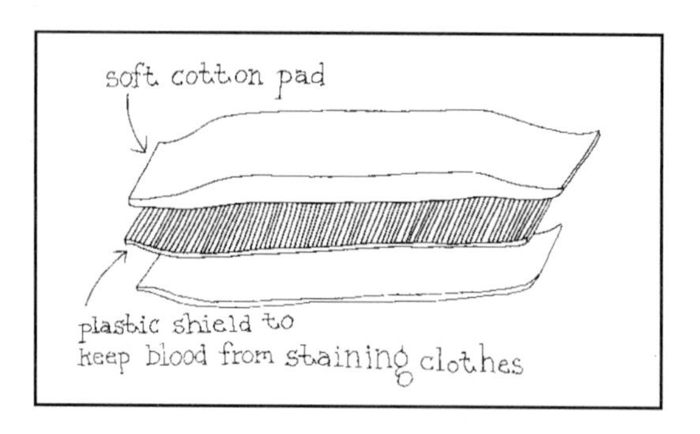

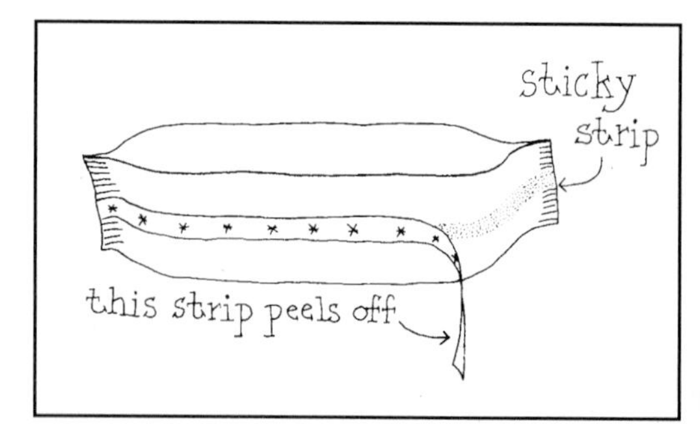

Pads come in many thicknesses and styles so you can choose styles or types that are comfortable for you and your menstrual flow. Thicker and more absorbent ones (the names vary from maxi to super absorbent) are often used for day one, two and three of your period. Switching to a thinner style (panty shields or liners) on the last days as your flow is ending, is common. Some styles come with "wing side flaps" to prevent leakage on to your clothes.

The next time you are in a grocery store or drug store, start checking out at the various packages. You will begin to get an idea of what you might like to use. Pick up a different package each time you are there and read what is on the package. Even if you don't have your period yet, but some of your friends do, you will understand what they are talking about.

It's true that for most girls, a pad feels funny at first. But pads fit close to your body and really don't show. If a large pad isn't comfortable, try a smaller size. (Positioning the pad in the best spot for you will take a bit of experimenting but you'll get the hang of it with practice.)

"The first time I wore a pad, it felt so huge and bulky. I was sure everyone could tell I was having my period. I was surprised when I looked in the mirror and saw that the pad didn't show at all."

Pads should be changed at least twice a day, more often when your menstrual flow is heavy.

NO PADS ARE FLUSHABLE so they need to be disposed of in a way that is comfortable for you and doesn't bother or offend anyone else. The most common way to do this is to fold it in half and put it back in the empty wrapper, or wrap toilet paper around it. Then put it in a waste basket. In public bathrooms you should see a small, covered waste container in each bathroom stall for that reason.

You might want to try on a pad before you ever start your period. This way, you can find out how to put one on and what it's like to wear one. It might be uncomfortable or awkward at first, but planning ahead may clear up confusions now rather than on the first day of your period.

Experiment. If you wear a pad that feels very bulky and uncomfortable, try a mini-pad. They're smaller and might be better for you. *You* decide what's best for your body.

TAMPONS

Tampons are another product used to catch menstrual blood before it leaves your body. They don't stop the menstrual flow. They absorb it. They are made of soft material pressed together into this kind of shape:

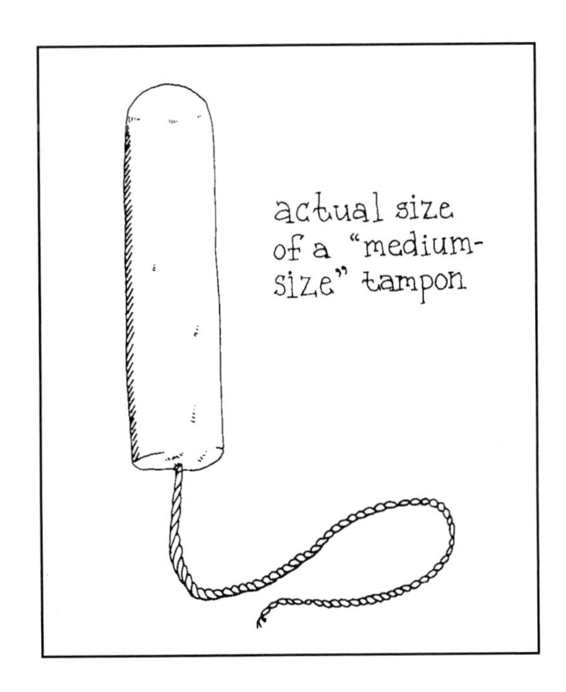

There is a string at the end of the tampon. Tampons fit inside the vagina and the string hangs down through the vaginal opening. When you want to remove a tampon, you pull gently on the string and it comes right out.

Tampons, like pads, come in different sizes. There are junior *(small)*, regular *(medium)*, super *(large)* and extra large *(superplus)* sizes. The first time you try a tampon, a smaller size (*slender or junior)* will probably be the easiest. A tampon with a rounded applicator tip is a good one to use at first.

Some tampons come with an applicator which helps guide the tampon into the vagina. It's thrown away when the tampon's in place. There are cardboard, plastic and stick applicators.

Some tampons don't have any applicator. You just use your finger to guide the tampon into your vagina. A good habit to get into is to wash your hands before inserting a new tampon. Of course, you will wash your hands afterwards whether using a tampon or a pad.

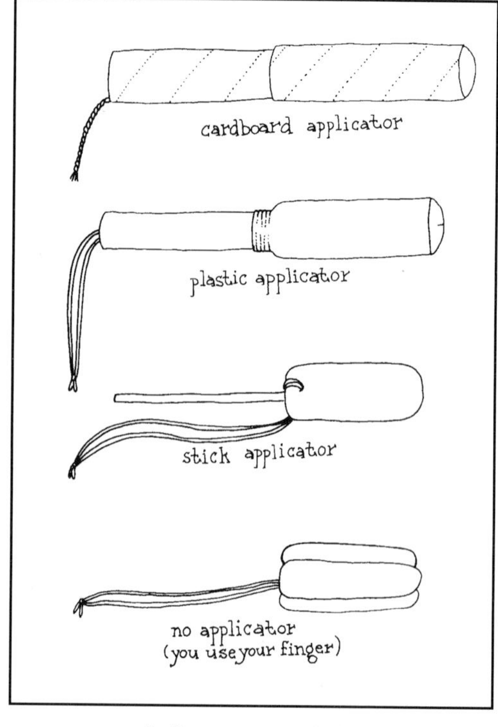

And, yes, virgins or girls who haven't had sex can use tampons.

If a tampon is put in the right way, you probably won't be able to feel it at all, but the first time may be confusing.

Everyone feels awkward learning to use a tampon. There are directions included in every box of tampons. Be sure you read them carefully if you're not sure how. You can also talk with your mother or with a friend who has used tampons before. *(The main trick is to aim toward the bottom of your spine rather than up towards your belly button.)*

If you do use tampons, it is important to change them at least four times a day (every four to six hours). You might want to use tampons during the day and a pad while you sleep. Some prefer to do just the opposite.

Some girls are afraid they might lose a tampon inside their vagina. A tampon really can't get lost inside of you—there's nowhere for it to go. The opening to the uterus is too small for a tampon to get through and the muscles of the vagina keep it from falling out. But on occasion, some have forgotten to take out the last tampon. Be sure you remember to remove your last one at the end of your period.

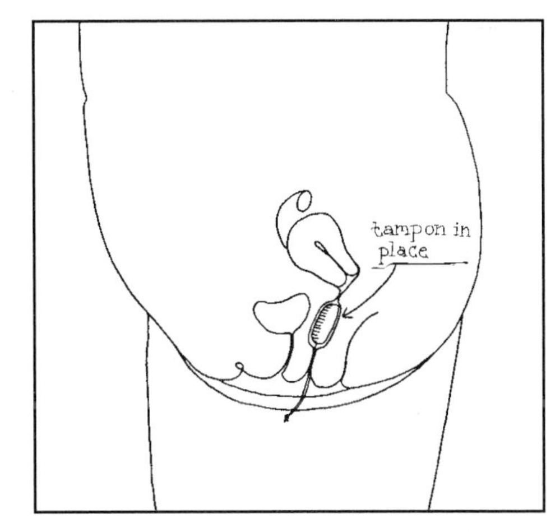

Most girls use pads when they first begin their periods. Later you might want to try tampons. The most important thing is for you to be comfortable with your choice. Each girl will find the product that suits her best.

Most tampons and their applicators can be flushed down the toilet. If the applicator is not biodegradable (plastic, for instance) or if you know that the toilet you are using has "flushing" problems, then you need to take the used item, wrap it up in toilet paper or tissues and throw it away. Every tampon package will tell you if the applicator is flushable or not.

Tampons do not have to be changed every time you use the toilet but some women do it more often than not.

There is a rare disease called Toxic Shock Syndrome (TSS). Not very many people have ever gotten this disease. The symptoms look like a very bad flu and it comes on very fast. But most women and girls who have had TSS got it because they did not change their tampons often enough. To make sure you stay healthy, change your tampons every four to six hours. If you have to go to a doctor with a very bad flu when you have your period and you are using tampons, let your doctor know you are using one so you can be checked for TSS. Girls and women using menstrual pads during their periods instead of tampons do not need to worry about this disease.

OTHER PRODUCTS

There are other products that some women use besides pads or tampons that they feel are better for the environment or better for their bodies. These are items like washable pads or protection/collection cups. After your period has become regular and you are comfortable using pads or tampons, you may wish to learn about and try one of these methods. Most people are happy using pads and tampons and, because they are available everywhere, you should know how to use them first.

If you are ever caught without pads or tampons when your period begins, remember that you can roll toilet paper around fingers 2-5 several times and make your own temporary pad. Even folded paper towels or a stack of paper napkins wrapped in toilet paper can work in an emergency.

If you are in school and you have nothing with you, just go visit the school nurse. They will have supplies available for you.

"Once I started my period very late Sunday night and I didn't have any pads or tampons. I got a clean washcloth and folded it so it would comfortably fit me, and used it like a pad. I just rinsed it out in cold water the next morning. It worked very well."

PHY.ED.

CHAPTER FIVE

I Have a Question About That

Menstruation is a big event in our lives. How we feel about it depends on what our mothers, friends, older sisters, grandmothers or aunts have said. If no one talks about menstruation, it can be very puzzling.

Bodies go through many changes, especially during the teens, and it can help to know what to expect. It's normal to have questions about menstruation. Many girls wonder how old they will be when they begin their periods or how they will know they have started menstruating.

Beginning to menstruate is a unique experience. No one can say exactly what it's going to be like for you, but the more you know about menstruation, the easier it will be.

Menstruation is as normal and natural for girls and women as eating or sleeping. It's a sign that we're changing and it happens at different times for all of us. Some girls begin to menstruate when they are quite young—maybe nine or ten years old. Others don't begin until they are sixteen or seventeen.

WHEN CAN I EXPECT TO GET MY PERIOD?

Because everyone's body is different, menstruation starts at different times. Most girls begin menstruating by twelve or thirteen but you may start as early as nine or ten or as late as fifteen or sixteen. It's not better to begin menstruating at one age or another. It doesn't mean you're more grown up if you start your periods at age ten, or immature if you start at eighteen. Usually your body knows just the perfect time for *you* to begin menstruating.

HOW MUCH BLOOD DO I LOOSE?

The amount of blood varies from girl to girl, especially during the first couple years of menstruation. A girl may lose as little as one tablespoon of blood or up to six tablespoons in each cycle. Your blood doesn't come out all at once. It dribbles and drips out, and a menstrual period may last from two to eight days. Even though you don't loose a lot of blood, it may seem that way to you. The blood may be red or it may look brownish.

Some girls lose more blood on the first day and less on the following days. Some bleed more on the second day. Some blood may come out in small clumps too. That is nothing to worry about. The way each girl menstruates is different.

WHAT DO I DO WHEN I GET MY PERIOD THE FIRST TIME?

You will probably discover this when you go to the bathroom. Or you may feel wet between your legs in a different kind of way.

If you discover this while you are at school, here are some suggestions:

The first thing you'll want to do is excuse yourself from class. Let your teacher know it is important that you leave the room. If you carry a purse and happen to have a pad with you, everything should be fine. You have probably practiced beforehand and will already know how to use it.

If you don't have a pad with you, your school might have a machine in the girl's bathroom that sells them. Check on what they cost so that you always have that amount of change with you. But, what if your school doesn't have a machine, or the machine is empty? Usually, the nurse's office will have sanitary pads available for situations like this, so try there next. Or check with a girl friend who might have an extra. You can also keep some in your locker.

If only a little blood has gotten on your underpants, you can probably wait until you get home to wash them out. Roll toilet paper around your fingers to "create" a temporary pad or do the same with some paper towels. Tying a sweater or jacket around your waist can hide any other stains.

If you get your first period at home, it will still be a big surprise. You might wake up in the morning with it or just discover it in a routine trip to the bathroom. Do you know where your mother's or sister's supplies are? Are there pads available as well as tampons? It is perfectly fine to call out and ask for help. Your first period will probably be short and not too heavy.

Once you have started menstruating, you will have a better idea of when your period will begin each month. You can be prepared by carrying a pad with you, but if your period ever surprises you, the few steps just mentioned should help out.

You will also discover good ways to be private about carrying around a pad or tampon when you are expecting your period. Pockets in sweaters or pants become important. Small containers like an eyeglass case or a small drawstring bag may work best for you.

WHAT IS A REGULAR CYCLE?

Your body goes through many changes, especially during the teens when you begin to menstruate. You will find it may take several years for your cycle to balance out and get used to this new process going on inside of you. This means you might miss a period for one month or even for six months in the beginning. You may have heavy bleeding one month and then hardly any at all the next. In a few years your body will get into a rhythm and your period should come somewhere between every 26 to 32 days, or approximately once a month. Many books say that women's menstrual cycles come every 28 days, but this is just an average and not the "right" length of time.

A good way to keep track of your period is by marking the days you menstruate on a calendar. (See page 74-75.) You will get an idea of how long you menstruate as well as how many days there are between periods. Menstrual cycles are measured from the day one period begins to the day the next period begins. Once you've started menstruating, if it seems that your cycle isn't regular after two years, you may want to tell somebody (your mother or someone else you feel comfortable with), and see a doctor.

Even when your cycle becomes regular, most women notice over the years that how their period feels to them changes as does the nature of their menstrual flow as well as how they feel about getting their period changes, too.

WHAT ABOUT CRAMPS?

Girls and women may get cramps or stomach pain when they menstruate. Cramps can hurt. Some have uncomfortable cramps while others hardly feel any difference at all when they menstruate. Cramps happen when your uterus, which is a muscle, contracts, similar to the way the muscles in your arm will tighten up (or contract) when you make a fist.

If you do get cramps, there are several things you can do that might help.

- Warmth causes muscles to relax and can help ease cramps. A hot water bottle or heating pad on your stomach may help. (But remember, hot water bottles and heating pads can cause burns if they're used for too long or they're too hot. Check it with someone else before using one to make sure you know how to use it correctly.) A warm bath may help too.

- Non-prescription painkillers (such as aspirin and its other forms) can be helpful. Check with an adult first and discuss what dosage to take. If you find that these over-the-counter products work for you, you may even want to start taking them before you start getting cramps and continue with the medication every six to eight hours for at least two days. Pain studies show that starting pain relief BEFORE the discomfort begins can be more effective than waiting until you "need" it.

- Sometimes just rubbing or massaging your stomach can make you feel better. You might try lying on your back with your knees up. Move your knees in a small circle. This is a kind of massage, too.

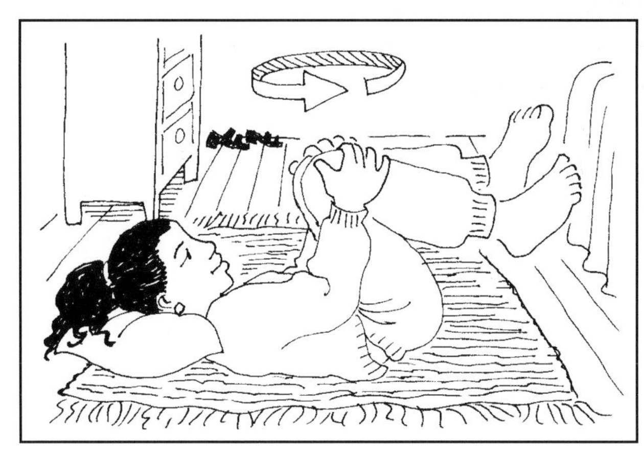

- Exercise that you generally do can keep blood flowing and may soon ease any discomfort.

- Taking a slow walk may help your cramps go away.

- Or just try crouching down in this position. It feels good because your uterus is hanging down, which helps it relax.

- Drinking something hot like tea or hot chocolate may make you feel better.

- Eating lightly before your period may help. This is because your intestines are packed into your body very close to your uterus. If you've eaten a food, your large intestines get filled up and take more room. Your uterus gets swollen during the first day or two or three of your period, so it takes up more room in the body. By eating lightly, you make more room for your uterus and it is less likely to cramp. Try it out sometime if you are having a lot of cramping.

- Whining to others may make you feel better—but probably not.

WHAT IS PMS?

PMS stands for pre-menstrual syndrome. As you hormones prepare your uterus to shed its lining, those same hormones can affect your emotional life, making you feel more sensitive, maybe sad or just grumpy. Some women are more affected by PMS than others.

WHAT KIND OF EXERCISE CAN I DO DURING MY PERIOD?

When you menstruate, you should do what feels right for you. Some of us can do anything we want when we're menstruating. Some of us can't. Since we're all so different, we have to decide what's best for our own bodies. After all, no one knows your body better than you do.

Some people say that it isn't a good idea to go swimming when you are menstruating. Swimming isn't harmful at all. Cool water may make you stop bleeding for awhile and hot water (like a hot bath) may make you bleed a little more heavily. Swimming is okay if you feel like it.

Wearing a tampon is the only choice if swimming. It is not appropriate to go in the water unless you are wearing a tampon for sanitary reasons.

Remember, whatever you do during your period, whether it's playing basketball, reading a book or swimming, really depends on how you feel. There's no right or wrong as long as you do what's comfortable for your body.

ISN'T THIS A SMELLY PROBLEM?

You may have heard that when you have your period, you have an odor about you that other people can smell. Because heat and air and odors float upwards, we're usually the only ones who can smell our own menstrual blood (if we smell it at all). Actually your menstrual flow has no odor until it comes into contact with air.

You may think you're smelly and bothering everyone who comes within two feet of you, but that's because you're so aware of yourself—not because you smell.

As long as you wash your genital area with soap and water as usual (or more often if you want to), and change your pad or tampon when necessary, you probably won't have any problems with odor. (When drying off with a towel, you might prefer to dry the area between your legs with toilet paper rather than your towel.)

WHAT IS A DOUCHE?

You may see ads in magazines about vaginal sprays and *douches* (DOOSH-es). A *douche* (DOOSH) is a liquid used to wash the vagina. Vaginal sprays are supposed to help keep you "clean and fresh" but it's been found that, for many women, sprays actually cause infections or rashes. Your vagina cleans itself naturally (like your eyes). The only reason for using a douche is if you have a medical problem and a doctor or nurse practitioner suggests you douche.

WHAT ABOUT REMOVING STAINS IN MY CLOTHES?

During your period, you might get some blood on your underpants. This is very common. With blood stains, use cold water to rinse clothes first. It works really well. Then plain old soap and water should get them clean.

Another excellent liquid for releasing blood stains is hydrogen peroxide poured on the stain area. Then rinse and wash as usual. You could use bleach as a last resort, especially with old stains.

If you know you tend to leak on heavy days, that's a good reason to wear jeans or dark colored skirts on those days.

I DON'T LIKE TALKING ABOUT THIS

Sometimes getting our period makes us proud, sometimes embarrassed. Girls who get it before their other friends are embarrassed. Girls who are last to get their period are embarrassed. You are not the first one to feel like this. Actually, we have all felt like this. This is normal.

It might be interesting for you to find out similar experiences your mother or friends had when they began menstruating. Sometimes it's comforting to talk to someone when something new is happening to you and you feel like you're the only one in the whole world who is different. The same goes for menstruation—the more we talk to people, the more we find out that our experiences, feelings and thoughts can be similar.

I'LL DIE IF ANYONE SEES ME BUYING A PACKAGE OF PADS

In the beginning going into a store to buy pads or tampons is awkward or embarrassing. It feels like everyone is watching you, especially the boys. But, like anything we do again and again, it's not such a big deal after awhile. It is a sign to anyone of your growing up and that is nothing to be ashamed of.

HOW OTHERS HAVE FELT

"I grew up in a small town, so I knew everyone who worked at the drugstore. It was awful for me to have to buy pads from people I knew so I always asked my mother to buy them for me."

"When I began menstruating, my mother told my older brothers, my father, and even the neighbors! Even now I feel sort of embarrassed when I menstruate."

"When I had cramps one day, several of my friends thought I was acting silly because I didn't want to go get some ice cream with them. They made me feel embarrassed only because I was trying to take care of myself. Now that I think about it, I was silly, but only for letting them make me feel embarrassed."

"For me, having my period was never any big deal. I've never had bad cramps and menstruation doesn't slow me down a bit. I still run and work and do everything I always do. If anything, I guess I have a little more energy during my period than at other times."

"I used to hate it when I got my period. But now I think of menstruation as my body telling me that everything inside of me is working and that I'm healthy."

Chapter Six

Why Do I Feel This Way?

As we grow older, we are able to see many changes in our bodies and sometimes our feelings and emotions are changing, too. It's natural to have new ideas and feelings at different times in our lives, but because you can't see or touch them, emotions can be confusing.

You may find when you start menstruating that your period affects the way you feel. There are different kinds of feelings girls and women may have and, like so many other things, no two people feel exactly the same.

We talked to a lot of women and girls who menstruate and asked them how they feel just before, during or after their periods, and here's what some of them said:

"I always love to take walks in the woods or along the beach, especially when I'm on my period."
– Jennifer

"Usually, I don't mind spending an evening alone, but around the time I menstruate, I feel very lonely if people aren't always around me."
– Lyn

"I like to take care of myself a lot when I'm having my period. I dress up or buy a new scarf or something."
– Amy

"Oh, I always feel so ugly at that time of the month. My face usually breaks out and I don't like that at all."
– Lisa

"I seem to have so little energy the first day of my period."
– Emily

"I have more energy than ever about the time I start my period."
– Dolores

"I can get so *mad sometimes about such little things. Right around the time I menstruate, my temper is very short."*
– Yvette

"Sometimes I feel like no one understands anything I'm trying to say."
– Gloria

"If I have time, I always love to bake bread when I'm having my period."
– Esther

"I write better poems when I'm menstruating."
—Roxanne

"Seems like I spend a lot of time thinking about serious things, especially when I'm menstruating."
– Toni

"When I'm having my period, I feel like I'm just one part of this big exciting world. My menstrual cycle makes me feel like part of the world's cycles – seasons, day and night. It's nice."
– Carol

"I get hungry for certain foods a day or two before my period. I'll get a real craving for scrambled eggs or strawberries and I'll raid the refrigerator late at night."
– Laura

There's no one way you *have* to feel or are *supposed* to feel when you're menstruating. Your period might not make you feel any different at all. Once again, part of what's so wonderful about us is that we are all so different about many things.

Chapter Seven

What is a Pelvic Exam?

A *pelvic* (PELL-vick) exam is an exam where a doctor or another medical worker checks the female organs inside and outside our bodies. It is sometimes called an internal exam. A nurse practitioner, your regular doctor or a gynecologist can do this exam. A *gynecologist* (GUY-nuh-KOL-oh-jist) is a doctor specially trained to take care of these female parts.

It is a good idea to have a pelvic exam when you turn 18 or if you have become sexually active, which ever comes first. Just like regular visits to the dentist, having a pelvic exam is very important. By the time you are an adult woman, you should have a pelvic exam every year. It is always better for your body to be checked regularly instead of waiting until you're sick. Regular check-ups can prevent sickness, and that's important!

Now you may only be seeing your regular doctor or nurse practitioner every other year. Let him or her know that you have started your period. This will NOT be a reason to have a pelvic exam, however.

If you are having menstrual problems, then your doctor may want you to have a pelvic exam to be sure there is no reason for concern. What are considered menstrual problems? If any of these are common for you after a year or two of menstruating, tell your doctor:

- You stop getting your period, or it only happens now and then.
- You're having incredibly, difficult cramps.
- You are menstruating every week or two and your flow is very heavy. Heavy means soaking a regular or maxi pad in an hour or two.

YOUR FIRST VISIT

Your first pelvic exam doesn't have to be a scary experience, especially if you know what is going on before it happens.

When you call for an appointment, it is okay to ask for a woman doctor or health professional, if that is important to you. And let them know that this is your first pelvic exam.

At the doctor's office or clinic, you will be asked to fill out a medical history. For instance, a doctor will want to know what diseases you or your family have had, the length of your menstrual period and the date of your last period. You might want to remind the nurse or doctor again that this will be your first pelvic exam.

If your mother or a girlfriend can go with you, it might make you feel better. If you'd like to have her go into the exam room with you, call ahead to make sure it's okay with your doctor. At the very least you can ask to have a health professional woman in the exam room with you. The doctor will probably say it's all right, but if not, and if it's important to you, you might want to find another doctor.

You will be asked to come into an exam room. Make sure you go to the bathroom before your exam. This will make the exam more comfortable for you. Once in the room, a nurse will ask you to undress and give you a paper dress to put on. You will be given a paper sheet also for extra coverage.

The nurse can explain to you how to put the dress on. Remember that no one looks good in these. They are used because they are disposable—not fashionable.

THE EXAM

After the doctor comes in the room and talks with you (everything discussed between the two of you is always private information that will not be shared unless it is life threatening), you will probably be asked to sit or lie down on the examining table. The doctor will first examine your breasts. This is done by gently pressing all around your breasts. You are being checked for any abnormal lumps or breast tissues that might be signs of disease. You may be shown how to do a breast exam yourself. If not, ask how to do it. You'll need to be able to check your breasts each month on your own.

After your breasts, your stomach area (*your abdomen*) will be checked.

INTERNAL EXAM

Next, your genitals and internal organs will be checked. You will be asked to lie down and put your feet on something called "stirrups." One kind is made so your feet rest on them. Another kind of stirrups is made so the backs of your knees rest on them. Your knees and legs will be spread open so the genital area is easier to see.

For many girls and women, this is the most embarrassing part of the exam. We're just not used to showing a very delicate and private part of ourselves, especially to strangers. This part of the exam might be easier for you if you go to a woman doctor or a nurse practitioner. But don't forget, whether it's a woman or a man, your doctor has done this thousands of times. It may be new to you, but he or she is used to it and is only concerned with your health.

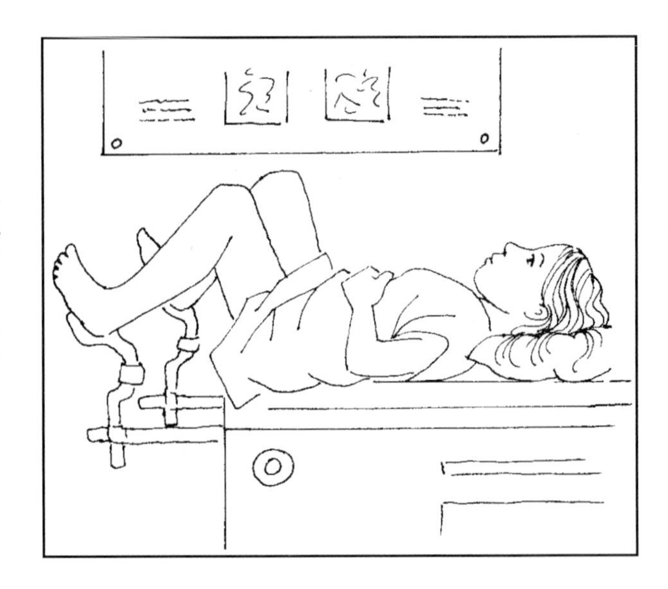

PAP SMEAR

The doctor will first look at your outside genitals to see that everything is healthy. Then your internal organs will be checked. To do this, a doctor will use a *speculum* (SPECK-you-lum). A speculum is either metal or plastic.

It is gently inserted into your vagina to hold the vaginal walls apart so the doctor can see inside. You will feel the pressure. It may be a bit uncomfortable but it should not be painful. Taking a slow, deep, in-and-out breath at this point can help you relax which, in turn, will help your vaginal muscles relax, making the whole process easier.

Then something called a Pap smear is taken. A cotton swab is gently touched in your cervical opening through the speculum to collect some of your cervical tissue cells. You probably won't feel this at all. These cells are put on a glass slide and sent to a laboratory. The Pap smear is a check to make sure the cells in your cervix are growing normally. Then the speculum will be removed.

Next, the doctor, wearing a pair of thin rubber gloves, applies a special slippery gel to his or her fingers. One finger will be inserted into your vagina and the other hand will press down on your stomach. This is the best way to see if your uterus, cervix, ovaries and fallopian tubes feel normal and healthy.

This whole exam will not take more than five minutes.

YOUR HEALTH PARTNER

The most important thing to remember about gynecology is to have anything that seems unusual checked out. If you have been feeling anything different around your genitals, like burning or itching or seeing a new kind of discharge (fluid which comes from your vagina), tell your gynecologist.

If your breasts hurt or you have any lumps in them, ask your doctor about it. Often when a girl's breasts are growing, there is some tenderness, but a doctor will be able to make sure everything is all right.

The more you tell your doctor, the better and more complete exam he or she will be able to give you. The better your exam is, the healthier you will be and, after all, that's what we all want from our pelvic exams.

WRITE IT DOWN

If you have any questions, ask them during your exam. You might even want to make a list to take into the room with you so you don't forget anything. Doctors sometimes don't give much information unless you ask. They've done this so many times before and don't realize that you might not know all about it yourself. But remember, it's your body, and you have every right to learn as much as you want about it.

If you are not comfortable asking questions or you don't feel your doctor is really listening to you, you may want to change doctors for your next exam.

Conclusion

Well, here we are at the end of this book. We hope you enjoyed looking at the pictures and that it answered many of your questions. There are two important things we'd like you to remember.

One is that no two people are ever quite the same.

The other is that we want you to ask questions and get answers to the things about your life that you don't understand.

After reading this book, you know more about menstruation than we knew when we were nine or ten years old. We learned a lot about menstruation just writing the book, and when we talked with some of our friends (both young girls and older women) we found that often they didn't know about some of these things, either. We hope that knowing how your body works makes growing up and going through all these changes easier.

Good luck!

About This Book

The first edition of *Period.* was written many years ago and was the first book available in bookstores on this topic for young girls. It has sold hundreds of thousands of copies and now has been updated and revised for the next generation of young women who still have many of the same questions that their mothers had when they read this book.

About the Original Authors

JoAnn (Gardner-)Loulan has been in private practice as a psychotherapist in the San Francisco Bay Area. She is a mother, author and lecturer. She authored books, chapters for anthologies and articles on topics of sexuality and self-esteem. Her lecturing has taken her all over the U.S., Canada and parts of Europe. Her mothering has taken her everywhere.

Bonnie (Lopez) Worthen previously worked as a facilitator in women's sexuality groups. Now she and her husband spend most of their time living and traveling in Europe and Asia while working on several new writing projects. She is the mother of two adult children, a son and a daughter.

Marcia Quackenbush, a licensed Marriage, Family & Child Counselor, has been active in HIV and AIDS work since 1984. She continues writing on health issues of importance to families.

Index

M

N

O

P

Q

S

T

U

V

W

This is your page. Use it as your record keeper.
Leave it in the book or tear it out.

FOR THE RECORD

ON THIS _____ DAY of _________(month) of 20____

I, _______________________________________(name),
living at:

____

____

and a student at _____________________________

found at ___________ (time)

and ____________________________________ (place)

at the age of _____ that I had begun my first period.

My best friend(s) are _____________________________

News headlines of the day _________________________

I felt ____

____

If you use this calendar *(or a photocopy of it)* for several months, you'll see how your cycle is working for you. Just mark a 'P' on your period days.

JAN	FEB	MARCH	APRIL	MAY	JUNE
1. ______	1. ______	1. ______	1. ______	1. ______	1. ______
2. ______	2. ______	2. ______	2. ______	2. ______	2. ______
3. ______	3. ______	3. ______	3. ______	3. ______	3. ______
4. ______	4. ______	4. ______	4. ______	4. ______	4. ______
5, ______	5, ______	5, ______	5, ______	5, ______	5, ______
6. ______	6. ______	6. ______	6. ______	6. ______	6. ______
7. ______	7. ______	7. ______	7. ______	7. ______	7. ______
8. ______	8. ______	8. ______	8. ______	8. ______	8. ______
9. ______	9. ______	9. ______	9. ______	9. ______	9. ______
10. ______	10. ______	10. ______	10. ______	10. ______	10. ______
11. ______	11. ______	11. ______	11. ______	11. ______	11. ______
12. ______	12. ______	12. ______	12. ______	12. ______	12. ______
13. ______	13. ______	13. ______	13. ______	13. ______	13. ______
14. ______	14. ______	14. ______	14. ______	14. ______	14. ______
15. ______	15. ______	15. ______	15. ______	15. ______	15. ______
16. ______	16. ______	16. ______	16. ______	16. ______	16. ______
17. ______	17. ______	17. ______	17. ______	17. ______	17. ______
18. ______	18. ______	18. ______	18. ______	18. ______	18. ______
19. ______	19. ______	19. ______	19. ______	19. ______	19. ______
20. ______	20. ______	20. ______	20. ______	20. ______	20. ______
21. ______	21. ______	21. ______	21. ______	21. ______	21. ______
22. ______	22. ______	22. ______	22. ______	22. ______	22. ______
23. ______	23. ______	23. ______	23. ______	23. ______	23. ______
24. ______	24. ______	24. ______	24. ______	24. ______	24. ______
25. ______	25. ______	25. ______	25. ______	25. ______	25. ______
26. ______	26. ______	26. ______	26. ______	26. ______	26. ______
27. ______	27. ______	27. ______	27. ______	27. ______	27. ______
28. ______	28. ______	28. ______	28. ______	28. ______	28. ______
29. ______	29. ______	29. ______	29. ______	29. ______	29. ______
30. ______		30. ______	30. ______	30. ______	30. ______
31. ______		31. ______		31. ______	

Once you've tracked your periods for awhile, you can move to just marking 'P' on your daily school or family calendar so you'll know when your last period started.

JULY	AUG	SEPT	OCT	NOV	DEC
1. ______	1. ______	1. ______	1. ______	1. ______	1. ______
2. ______	2. ______	2. ______	2. ______	2. ______	2. ______
3. ______	3. ______	3. ______	3. ______	3. ______	3. ______
4. ______	4. ______	4. ______	4. ______	4. ______	4. ______
5, ______	5, ______	5, ______	5, ______	5, ______	5, ______
6. ______	6. ______	6. ______	6. ______	6. ______	6. ______
7. ______	7. ______	7. ______	7. ______	7. ______	7. ______
8. ______	8. ______	8. ______	8. ______	8. ______	8. ______
9. ______	9. ______	9. ______	9. ______	9. ______	9. ______
10. ______	10. ______	10. ______	10. ______	10. ______	10. ______
11. ______	11. ______	11. ______	11. ______	11. ______	11. ______
12. ______	12. ______	12. ______	12. ______	12. ______	12. ______
13. ______	13. ______	13. ______	13. ______	13. ______	13. ______
14. ______	14. ______	14. ______	14. ______	14. ______	14. ______
15. ______	15. ______	15. ______	15. ______	15. ______	15. ______
16. ______	16. ______	16. ______	16. ______	16. ______	16. ______
17. ______	17. ______	17. ______	17. ______	17. ______	17. ______
18. ______	18. ______	18. ______	18. ______	18. ______	18. ______
19. ______	19. ______	19. ______	19. ______	19. ______	19. ______
20. ______	20. ______	20. ______	20. ______	20. ______	20. ______
21. ______	21. ______	21. ______	21. ______	21. ______	21. ______
22. ______	22. ______	22. ______	22. ______	22. ______	22. ______
23. ______	23. ______	23. ______	23. ______	23. ______	23. ______
24. ______	24. ______	24. ______	24. ______	24. ______	24. ______
25. ______	25. ______	25. ______	25. ______	25. ______	25. ______
26. ______	26. ______	26. ______	26. ______	26. ______	26. ______
27. ______	27. ______	27. ______	27. ______	27. ______	27. ______
28. ______	28. ______	28. ______	28. ______	28. ______	28. ______
29. ______	29. ______	29. ______	29. ______	29. ______	29. ______
30. ______	30. ______	30. ______	30. ______	30. ______	30. ______
31. ______	31. ______		31. ______		31. ______

PERIOD.

A Parent's Guide

Talking With Your Children

A Parent's Guide

BOOK PEDDLERS
15245 Minnetonka Blvd Minnetonka, MN 55345
952-912-0036 • fax: -952-912-0105
www.bookpeddlers.com

To order this Parent's Guide, alone, in quantity,
please contact the publisher.

TALKING ABOUT MENSTRUATION WITH YOUR CHILDREN

Topics concerning our bodies and their development, pregnancy and conception, menstruation and growing up are a constant source of interest and learning for our children. They want to know about the nitty-gritty aspects of bodily development: smells, fluids, "bad words," what a tampon feels like in your vagina, whether menstruation hurts. They giggle or make faces—"Oh, yuck!"—but they love to know the answers.

Children also learn things in stages, sometimes in very small steps. They remember information they use regularly and forget things that don't seem as important. This is why so many parents who feel they have already thoroughly covered certain topics find basic questions coming up over and over again. Talking with our children about "growing up" is something parents can do for their children throughout their lives. It will never be covered in one or two well-timed discussions. This is a matter we can bring into our children's lives on a regular basis.

WHO BEGINS?

Children benefit from hearing about growing up from many different adults. Mothers, fathers, grandparents, aunts and uncles, good family friends—all may have something to contribute to a child's understanding. Each family will be different in how they go about sharing this information.

WHAT'S THE RIGHT AGE TO SHARE INFORMATION?

The best time is obviously BEFORE menses starts. The surprise arrival of vaginal bleeding is scary for the unprepared. Studies also show that puberty is beginning earlier and earlier each decade. Today, girls usually go through puberty between the ages of nine and sixteen; boys between ten and seventeen. African-American girls are known to start a year earlier, on average. By eight or nine years of age, girls are usually curious and probably starting to talk amongst themselves.

Whenever your child brings up the subject is also the right time.

Every child matures on a different schedule. Watch your child's other signs of maturation as a guide to bringing up the topic, signs such as breast development, pubic hair, vaginal discharge. What can be too early for one can be too late for another.

If you're divorced, it is helpful if you let the other parent know if the topic has come up and how you've handled it. Mom, if a 10-14 year old daughter will be spending time with dad either on weekends or for the summer, let dad know he may want to have some supplies on hand. Or encourage your daughter to keep some items there. They will come in handy...eventually.

WHAT ABOUT THE BOYS?

Period. was written specifically for premenstrual girls, but we know parents who have bought the book for their young sons. Often menstruation gets left out of their education and becomes a mysterious event. If you have sons, be sure to tell them about how they will change as they grow up, and talk to them also about the changes girls go through.

In the beginning of *Period.* we talk about how magazines and movies make everyone look beautiful and perfect, as if they have no problems at all. Parent guides sometimes do the same thing, and a parent can easily feel like something is wrong if his or her children won't talk about growing up, even when the suggestions in the books and magazine articles are followed. We know how hard these things can be, and we've made lots of mistakes with our own children. But one of the things we've also found is if you keep trying and you don't have unrealistic expectations of yourself or your children, you can have some rewarding experiences together.

THE VOICE OF THE PARENT

"I gave a copy of Period. *to my niece, Amy, when she was six. She was so excited about it, she sat down right then and there to read the book. This was during a big family gathering—Amy's older sisters Lisa and Laura (seven and eight) where there. So were her young cousins Jenny and Adam (five and three). Add in Amy's parents, her grandparents, another aunt and uncle, and you can see we had quite a group.*

Well, all of us sat around the living room while Amy read the book out loud. When she came to a word that was hard to pronounce, or a concept that she couldn't understand, she would ask someone else in the room. We had three generations of the family there, all talking openly about menstruation and cramps, vaginas and tampons—it was great!

This wasn't something we had done before. It's not like we were the original liberal family and we always talked about these things. I am sure Amy's grandparents and parents were uncomfortable and a little embarrassed to be talking about matters that felt so private to them. But the children approached it openly with real excitement and that excitement was infectious. We all helped Amy learn about menstruation and growing up, and she helped all of us learn a new way to be together."

— JoAnn

"My wife and I divorced when our children were young and now we share custody. Generally, I see my kids one evening a week and on alternate weekends. And, honestly, I'm aware that I get to be the "fun parent," while my ex-wife has to deal with more of the day-to-day issues about chores and discipline and homework.

One of the men I work with mentioned something the other day about his eleven-year-old beginning to menstruate and I realized that my daughter Christie is nine now. I've sort of assumed all along that her mom would discuss these growing up issues with her and probably she has. But I don't know for sure, and even if her mom has, I don't really know what she has said to Christie. Like a lot of other divorced couples, we try to stay on top of things but our communication is not always great.

Well, I thought, why should I deprive my daughter of my feelings about growing up? I'd like her to hear about some of my experiences, and I really want to hear about hers. I talked this over with her mom and let her know I was going to have some talks of my own with Christie. Then I bought Christie a copy of Period. *and we started talking about it. It's hard for me sometimes, but it's really worth it because I have this whole new opportunity to get to know my daughter better."*

– Michael

"I remember using books and explaining to my son at some point between eight and ten how bodies work (including girls' menstruating) so he'd have the right information, not just what he picked up from other kids. His sister, three years younger, was given the same story at the equivalent age. Her older brother walked in while we were going through a book with drawings. I gulped for a moment but continued. He sat down with us and the discussion continued. Afterwards I realized what a gift he had given me—and hopefully, her too. Sex education now was something they would expect boys and girls to discuss in the same room. They would see this information as just matter-of-fact—something boys and girls discuss without giggles or embarrassment." — Vicki

Of course, stories like this tend to make it all sound pretty easy. You always hear about everyone's successes. When you think about bringing up these issues with your own children, the situation may seem very different from the experiences here.

"My daughter Tiffany is eleven—my age when I started to menstruate. I know she's had some education in school so it won't come as a total surprise to her but I want to talk to her about my own experiences too.

No one even talked about menstruation with me and I was terrified when I started my periods. Knowing my family, I'm sure it was the same for my mother and my grandmother.

I've read the suggestions in magazine articles about having books around and how to just start talking to your child and admit to your own discomfort or embarrassment. When I tried this, Tiffany tried to leave the room. 'Come back here, young lady,' I scolded, knowing this wasn't the way it was supposed to be going. 'I just wonder if you have any questions about these thing—menstruation, your body's changes—you know?'

'Mom! Please!' she wailed and wouldn't say another word. I had to let her go and she went and watched TV for the rest of the night. I just don't see how I can do this with my kid."

— Raelyn

SO WHAT CAN YOU EXPECT?

Most children are fairly selective about what they say to their parents. Some topics are easier to discuss than others. Many children who are eight or ten or twelve hardly talk to their parents about anything at all. Children these ages do spend a lot of time talking to their peers. And teen and preteen children are always embarrassed about *everything*. Don't let that stop you. If anything, that's a good reason to start these discussions earlier rather than later. Don't expect to fit everything into one discussion.

We may assume because they don't talk back to us, they aren't listening to what we have to say. This is not necessarily true. Most children are good listeners, and sometimes they are even "sly" listeners—overhearing things we would rather they not hear at all! But they also tend to have a short attention span, and they may be uncomfortable about how to respond to the things you say.

And what can you expect from yourself? Expect to feel awkward, expect to make mistakes, and expect to feel frustrated. When your "growing-up talk" with your child doesn't flow the nice easy way it did on a television sitcom last week, don't blame yourself. And most importantly, expect that this will get easier and better with practice.

HOW TO BEGIN

You can choose moments to talk to your child when you are in your car or on a plane, while you're preparing dinner together, or during a TV commercial. You might just say something about growing up. Start with a personal comment. "You're ten years old now. You know, when I was ten I started menstruating. I don't think we've ever even talked together about getting your period."

Don't expect a conversation, and don't put your child on the spot with questions. Make a few comments, and then move on to another topic if your child seems unprepared to have this discussion.

And once you've done that, what next? You may want some fresh material for a next short discussion. If you haven't already, read this book. Don't just set it in front of your child without knowing what it has to say. You might have different feelings and experiences other than in the book. Your experiences are unique. Share them with your children. And leaving this book in their room *(versus the kitchen table)* is another sensitive tact to take. There are lots of other possibilities:

- If you're a woman, talk about your own experiences beginning to menstruate—when you started, how it felt, how your family responded, and the sorts of things your friends said. Talk about the things your parents said—or didn't say. Bring up other memories of your childhood and adolescence having to do with growing up generally.
- If you're a man, talk about when you first learned about menstruation and what you and other boys your age thought and felt about it.
- Talk about advertisements about tampons, menstrual pads, feminine hygiene sprays, douches, etc. that you see in magazines or on TV.
- Describe the movies about menstruation you saw in your school. Ask about what they've been shown or lectured about.
- Talk about the myths you heard about menstruation while you were growing up. Ask your child if she has ever heard such things, and then correct them: *"You can't take baths during your period;" "You can't get pregnant while you're menstruating;" "You shouldn't go swimming during your period;" "Don't do any vigorous exercise;" "Cramps are imaginary;"* or *"Women are always irritable or nervous during their periods."*

These talks can be a fine opportunity to share some of your own vulnerabilities with your child. You can talk about the difficulties you faced as a young person, about times you were afraid or confused by your body's changes. You can let your child see that the two of you have had some similar experiences. By letting our children see that we have gone through these kinds of events, that we have survived and even learned from them, we are helping them learn that this is a normal process and that they will survive it too.

Over time, your child may feel more comfortable asking you questions and really discussing these things. But don't worry too much if she doesn't. She is listening to you, and your continued efforts demonstrate to her that these are important issues to you and that you care about her.

CREATE YOUR OWN RITE-OF-PASSAGE

Rituals are sorely missing in our culture. While not every girl will be open to making this occasion a celebration, it is worth marking the moment. Here is a wonderful opportunity to create a special memory for your daughter.

Before your daughter gets her period:

- Ask her to think about a special celebration with you that you'll carry out when she gets her first period. Would she like a family dinner, a slumber party with her girlfriends, a dinner at nice restaurant with you, tickets to a play?
- Use her tenth birthday (*a double digit coming-of-age*) for a special outing. It could be a mom-daughter dinner or lunch out, perhaps a small corsage and copy of *Period.* to herald her approaching womanhood.

- Take a trip to a local hospital and look at the newborn babies together, maybe even the hospital where she was born. For girls who have not been around tiny babies, this can be very exciting. It gives you another opportunity to talk about what she was like when she was an infant, the ways she has changed since then, and how she will continue to change as she matures and how, without getting a period, none of this would have happened. *(Wonderful for building self-esteem.)*

When a girl does get her period:

- Carry out that special celebration you planned. Maybe getting her ears pierced has been the agreed-upon event. It's a visible, yet secret, code to mark the occasion.
- Bring her a bouquet of flowers.
- Write your daughter a letter including some of your own memories of growing up and your feelings about how she is growing up. This becomes a keepsake—something she can read in private, look over again in the future, save with her special things—if she wants.
- Write her a poem to mark the event.
- Give her a book celebrating womanhood.
- Have a tea party for her with the other important women in her life.
- Remind her she can fill in *FOR THE RECORD* on page 73.

OTHER RESOURCES

This book, or any others on the topic from your library or bookstore, are always helpful. For starters, you can use the printed inserts in every package of tampons. They have a lot of information.

Let your daughter know there are product samples *(some free, some not)* she can send for, call for, or request from companys' internet sites. Or do it together.

For a free sample of Tampax® Satins, call 1-800-888-3115, or make your request, if you are over 13, at their website: www.tampax.com/suite. For $7.99, you can order *Always' Just Us Girls* Kit containing booklets and a sampling of pads, pantiliners and tampons, if you call 1-800-462-7500, or send a check or money order for that amount to: *Always' Just Us Girls Kit*, attn: Dan Lee, PO Box 141142, Cincinnati, OH 45250. Or you can order it on-line with a credit card, if you're over 13, at: www.pubertykit.com.

For a free sample of Playtex®tampons, visit their website at www.playtextampons.com. Playtex also offers the *Straight Talk. Period.* Video Kit, a 20-minute information video for mother and daughter accompanied by an informational booklet and a sample of Slimfit®tampons. This video kit costs $7.95 and can be ordered by visiting their website, calling toll-free 1-877-4-PLAYTEX, or sending a check to: Playtex, Straight Talk. Period., PO Box 1084, Grand Rapids, MN 55745-1084.

Internet sites offer a wealth of additional information. Teens will enjoy visiting www.troom.com, while you might find www.bodymatters.com or www.always.com of interest to you.

A PELVIC EXAM FOR YOUR DAUGHTER

It is certainly not necessary for a girl to have an pelvic exam upon getting her period, however, excessive cramping, bleeding or sporadic periods may be reasons. It can also be a gift to take her to a trusted doctor during her teen years, before she is sexually active or goes to work or off to college, so she knows how to do it on her own and gets in the habit of regular exams for her own health and welfare. If your daughter does pass sixteen without beginning menstruation, it is appropriate to consult with a doctor.

IT'S A GOOD THING

When you talk with your children, share with them your own sense of wonder at the ways they've grown and changed. Sit down with them and look over their baby pictures. Let them be inspired by your own pride in them, so they can feel good about themselves and the ways they are growing.

As you continue to talk about these things, you will find it easier to do. When you feel unsure, or frustrated, or intimidated, think about how you would act if you knew exactly what you were doing and felt totally confident. Then act as if this were actually the case. Acting “as if” is a great technique to get us past our stumbling blocks, and it really works.

Learn what your child’s health curriculum is—and when it covers what—in their school. Take advantage of community organizations and school programs about growing up. You can check with your church, a school nurse, local Planned Parenthood chapters, or community groups such as the Girls' Club, Girl Scouts, YWCA, etc. about what they offer.

Putting effort into open communication with our children always pays off. Sometimes we aren't sure what to say or do. It takes work on our part to give our children a legacy of pride and wonder in the workings of their bodies. What a truly precious gift we offer them when they can understand their changing bodies and delight in what is to come!